A Carriage Ride in Queen Square

Original compositions by Gwen Bevan,
great-great-granddaughter of Jane Austen's niece, Fanny Knight

Easy-to-play piano pieces for Jane Austen's Bath

with accompanying CD

Wyncliffe Books, Bath

I have written each of these dozen pieces to reflect a different aspect of Bath as Jane Austen would have known it.

For many years, I have been teaching the piano to children and adults. Sometimes pupils have found the edited versions of the classics not so enjoyable. So I have written these pieces to be tuneful and expressive without being too difficult; they also offer opportunities for learning technique. Although I had mainly adult learners in mind, both adults and children (boys as well as girls) have really enjoyed learning them.

Jane Austen did not marry, and there are no direct descendants. However I am the great great-granddaughter of her favourite niece Fanny Knight (right).

Gwen Bevan
Bath

Published by Wyncliffe Books
© Copyright 2009 Gwen Bevan
ISBN   978-0-9563292-0-2
ISMN   979-0-9002173-0-1

Contents

1 Great Pulteney Street

VIEWS IN THE CITY OF BATH

GREAT PULTNEY STREET.

R. Woodroffe. delt   On Stone by Giles.

Published by C. Duffield at his Gallery of Engravings. 12 Milsom St. Bath.

Printed by Day. 17 Gate Street.

"They arrived at Bath. Catherine was all eager delight – her eyes were here, there, everywhere, as they approached its fine and striking environs, and afterwards drove through those streets which conducted them to the hotel. She was come to be happy, and she felt happy already. They were soon settled in comfortable lodgings in Pulteney Street."

Northanger Abbey

Andante

(2nd time p cresc. poco a poco)

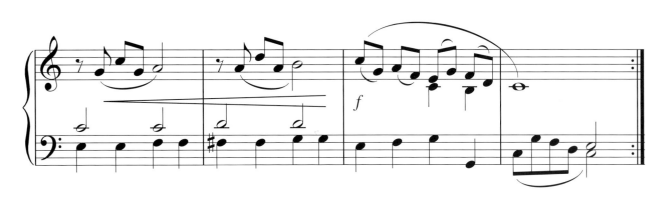

The Circus

The Circus was designed by John Wood in 1754, being influenced by Masonic concepts.

Although the centre was originally an open paved area, by the time Jane Austen came to Bath, a railed garden had been constructed.

The music reflects the circular movement.

Andante

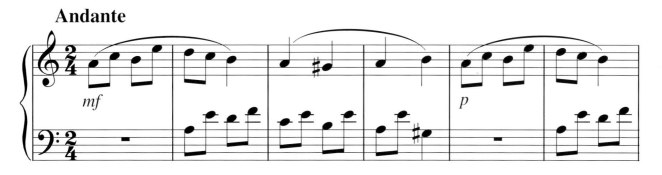

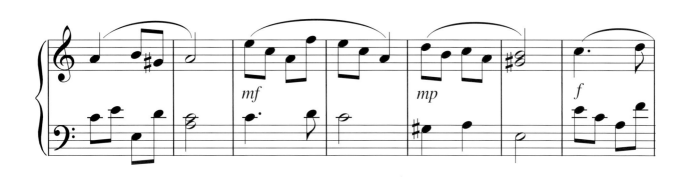

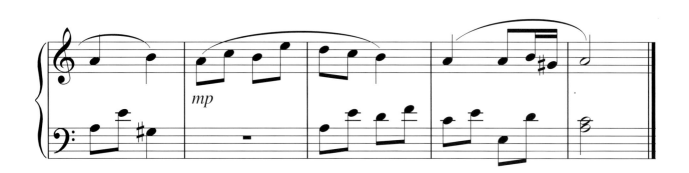

3 Working the Stone

Jane Austen's Bath was built with local stone. It has a wonderful distinctive hue, reflecting light in a variety of shades.

In the music you can hear the masons at work.

Allegro

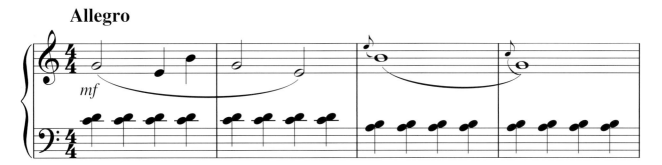

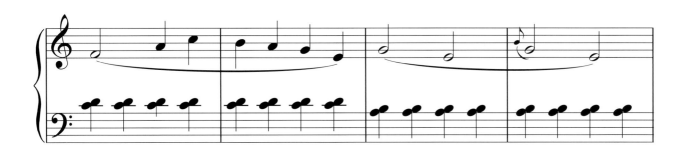

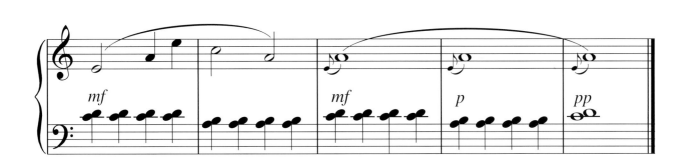

4 South Parade

The Parade, designed by John Wood, was built in the 1740s. The width allowed people to stroll in comfort, to see and to be seen. The music reflects this pastime.

When Jane Austen arrived in Bath, the family considered buying a place in South Parade, but Jane thought it was "too hot". Note the awnings over some windows.

Allegro

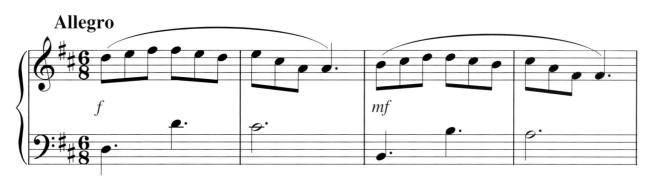

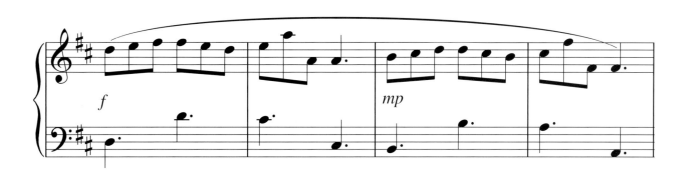

5 Sedan Chair

Sedan chairs were a common way of getting around the steep lanes of Bath in Jane Austen's time. They had right-of-way, and pedestrians had to flatten themselves against walls or railings to let the chairs past. They could even be carried inside into houses, the baths or the Pump Room.

Beau Nash licensed them like taxis and fixed the fares. A single trip within the city cost six pence (2.5p in today's money) and for a day's use it was four shillings (20p).

Andante

6 Sydney Gardens

Jane Austen often walked in Sydney Gardens. These were pleasure
gardens: "interspersed with a great number of small delightful groves
… decorated with waterfalls, stone and thatched pavilions … bowling
greens, swings and a labyrinth …"

New Bath Guide, 1801

The music reflects this relaxed atmosphere.

Leisurely

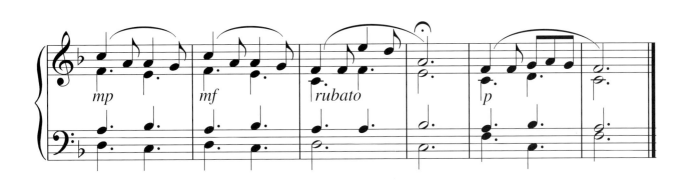

7   Gossip in the Pump Room

Drawn & Engraved by Rob.ᵗ Cruikshank.   *Published by Sherwood & Cᵒ. Octʳ. 1. 1825.*

Well known characters in the Pump Room, Bath, taking a sip with King Bladud.

"They all set off in good time for the Pump Room where the ordinary course of events took place. Mr Allen after drinking his glass of water, joined some gentlemen to talk over the politics of the day and compare the accounts of their newspapers; and the ladies walked about together noticing every new face and almost every new bonnet in the room."

Northanger Abbey

8   A Touch of Gout

"Lord Ringbone, who lay in the parlour below
On account of the gout he had got in his toe,
Began on a sudden to curse & to swear:
I protest my dear Mother, 'twas shocking to hear
The oaths of that reprobate gouty old Peer."

"Lord Ringbone, who lay in the parlour below,
On account of the gout he had got in his toe.
Began on a sudden, to curse and to swear:
I protest my dear Mother, 'twas shocking to hear.
The Oaths of that reprobate gouty old Peer."

Sneyd's illustration to Christopher Anstey's *The New Bath Guide*, c.1815

Andante

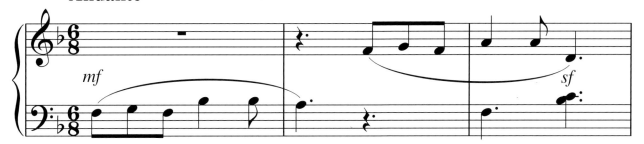

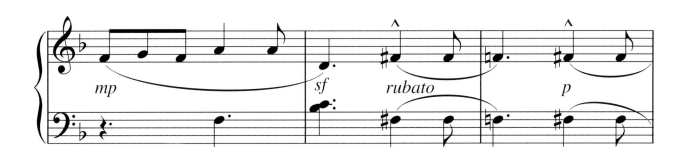

a tempo

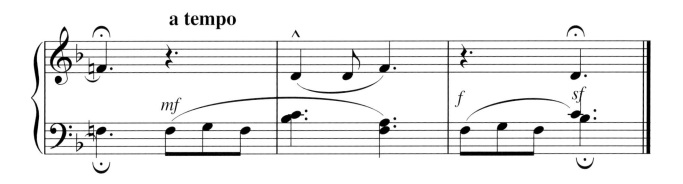

9 A Carriage Ride in Queen Square

Jane Austen took lodgings at Number 13 with her brother Edward and his family. She wrote to her sister Cassandra:

"We are exceedingly pleased with the House; the rooms are quite as large as we expected, Mrs Bromley is a fat woman in mourning, & a little black kitten runs about the Staircase."

Moderato

10 Admiring the Royal Crescent

Royal Crescent Bath,

"For a fine Sunday in Bath empties every house of its inhabitants and all the world would appear on such an occasion to walk about and tell their acquaintance what a charming day it is. So they hastened it to the Crescent to breathe the fresh air of better company."

Northanger Abbey

Con moto

Fine

D.C. al Fine

rit. _ _ _ _ _ _

11 Jacob's Ladder

BATH ABBEY CHURCH

In 1499, Bishop Oliver King came to Bath and had a dream about angels ascending and descending a ladder. It inspired him to rebuild the dilapidated Abbey.
The carvings on the west front commemorate his dream.

The music reflects the angels' actions.

11 Jacob's Ladder

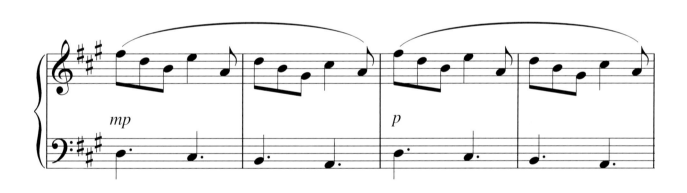

12 Alone on Beechen Cliff

"Beechen Cliff, that noble hill whose beautiful verdure and hanging coppice render it so striking an object from almost every opening in Bath."

Northanger Abbey

12 Alone on Beechen Cliff

Wistfully

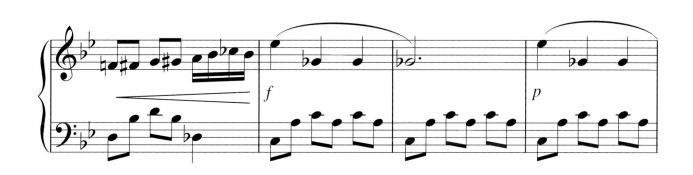

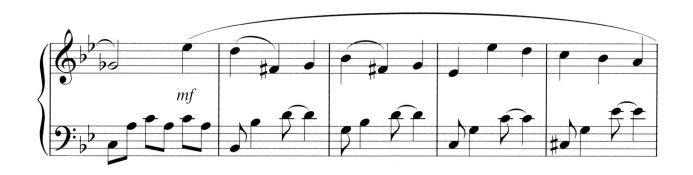

Acknowledgements

Page 4: Great Pulteney Street, c.1830.
www.bathintime.co.uk – Bath Central Library Collection.
Page 6: Circus with opening into Bennett Street.
Victoria Art Gallery, Bath and North East Somerset.
Page 8: Completion of the Royal Crescent, Bath.
Victoria Art Gallery, Bath and North East Somerset.
Page 10: The South Parade in Bath, 1784.
www.bathintime.co.uk – Bath Central Library Collection.
Page 12: Great Pulteney Street, c.1830.
www.bathintime.co.uk – Bath Central Library Collection.
Page 14: Joseph Basnett in a sedan chair, 1777.
www.bathintime.co.uk – Bath Central Library Collection.
Page 16: Well-known characters in the Pump Room, Bath,
taking a sip with King Bladud, 1825.
www.bathintime.co.uk – Bath Central Library Collection.
Page 18: Watercolour sketch for *Anstey's Bath Guide*, c.1815, No. 7.
www.bathintime.co.uk – Bath Central Library Collection.
Page 20: Queen's Square Bath, North Terrace.
Victoria Art Gallery, Bath and North East Somerset.
Page 22: Royal Crescent, Bath, 1804.
www.bathintime.co.uk – Bath Central Library Collection.
Page 25: Bath Abbey Church, 1822.
www.bathintime.co.uk – Bath Central Library Collection.
Page 29: South view of Bath, 1773.
Published 30 November 1773.
www.bathintime.co.uk – Bath Central
Library Collection.